# ADWORDS TOOLBOOK:

# Free Tools for Better PPC Advertising

## 2017 EDITION

BY JASON MCDONALD, PH.D.

© 2017 JM INTERNET GROUP

https://www.jm-seo.org/

"The perfect is the enemy of the good."

~ Voltaire

# 0

# INTRODUCTION

**PPC** or "**pay-per-click**" is a way of advertising most associated with Google AdWords. AdWords is far and away the dominant advertising platform on the Internet, though Facebook advertising is gaining ground, fast. That said, within PPC, we must also focus on Bing advertising, which is a look-alike platform to Google AdWords, running ads on both Bing and Yahoo.

This Toolbook is my compilation of the best, free tools to enhance your paid advertising on Google, Bing, and Yahoo. Also included are books, tutorials, and other resources that can help you learn, from many sources, the secrets to effective pay-per-click advertising.

## TO DO LIST:

» Understand How the *AdWords Toolbook* Works

» Register Your Copy Online

» Contents

» Acknowledge the Copyright and Disclaimer

» Write a Review, Get a Free eBook

## » UNDERSTAND HOW THE *ADWORDS TOOLBOOK* WORKS

First and foremost, the *AdWords Toolbook* assumes a **working knowledge of pay-per-click advertising**, in general, and Google AdWords, in particular. This Toolbook has many wonderful free tools, but the tools alone are useless without a knowledge of how the game is played! (If you need that knowledge, I recommend you check out my online courses at https://www.jm-seo.org/, or call 800-298-4065 to learn more about my AdWords one-on-one training and consulting services).

Second, this book emphasizes only **free** tools. Despite the fact that there are quite a few *paid* advertising tools out there, none are any better than the free tools identified in this *Toolbook*. Indeed, in today's tight economy, why pay when you can get them for free? Not to mention, why pay when the most important element, i.e. a knowledge of how AdWords is played to win, can't be obtained from any tool?

Third, I have reviewed each tool in the *Toolbook* for relevance and ease of use. Almost without exception, the tools in the *Toolbook* require nothing more than a Web browser and active connection to the Internet. *Easy* is just as important as *free*. Generally speaking, if a tool requires registration or has only a "trial" period, it has been excluded. A few paid tools have been included (e.g., call tracking services) when there are no reliable free alternatives.

## » REGISTER YOUR COPY ONLINE

If you've purchased this *Toolbook* in hard copy format, be aware that if you register online, you get instant access to a PDF copy, which has easy, clickable links to all resources. To do so, simply:

- Go to http://jmlinks.com/8d.
- Sign up as indicated.
- You'll be transferred to my "Dashboard" which includes all my tools – AdWords, SEO, and Social Media Marketing.
    - There, you'll have easy access to the BEST tools as identified herein.
    - You can also download a PDF copy of this *Toolbook* which can be read online and will have clickable links.

**Note**: *if you email me your Amazon receipt for this Toolbook, I will rebate you 50% of your cost once you sign up for the email alert system.*

## » TABLE OF CONTENTS

**Get More Free Stuff!**

You can find out about my other toolbooks, workbooks, and free resources by signing up for my email alerts at http://jmlinks.com/free.

Finally, the *Toolbook* is really mean to be read "online" rather than "on paper," since all of the links are clickable. As you read about an interesting tools, I encourage to click over and check each tool out. AdWords is a learn-by-doing art, and so are the tools!

Let's get started!

## ≫ ACKNOWLEDGE THE COPYRIGHT AND DISCLAIMER

platforms, *AdWords*. No endorsement by Google / Alphabet is implied or should be construed.

## Make Changes at Your Own Risk

Any changes that you or your organization make to your online advertising on Google AdWords and/or Bing and/or Yahoo, website content, link building, social media marketing, content, or any element of your Internet marketing and/or search engine optimization strategy or tactics are made your own risk. By downloading and using the *Toolbook* you are agreeing to the terms of service: you are completely responsible for all changes you may, or may not, make to your Internet marketing strategy.

## ≫ MEET THE AUTHOR

My name is Jason McDonald, and I have been active on the Internet since 1994 (*having invented the Internet along with Al Gore*) and taught SEO, AdWords, and Social Media since 2009 – online, at Stanford University Continuing Studies, at both AcademyX and the Bay Area Video Coalition in San Francisco, at workshops, and in corporate trainings across these United States. I love figuring out how things work, and I love teaching others! SEO is an endeavor that I understand, and I want to empower you to understand it as well.

Learn more about me at https://www.jasonmcdonald.org/ or at my corporate website https://www.jm-seo.org/. Or just call 800-298-4065, say something flattering, and I my secretary will put you through. (*Like I have a secretary! Just call if you have something to ask or say*).

# 1

# KEYWORDS

Keywords drive the process of advertising both from the searcher side (the *keyword query*) and from the advertiser side (the *keyword trigger*). Matching is "tight" on Google's Search Network as well as Bing / Yahoo, and "loose" on the Google Display Network. Whichever network you're on, you'll need a systematic keyword list. Here are my favorite tools with the best tools first.

**SEED KEYWORDS** - http://www.seedkeywords.com/

> This is a wonderful human / machine tool. Gather your team together (or they can be in diverse cities). Create a prompt, such as 'your hungry and you love Italian food, what would you search for?' This then creates a 'workspace' and as people type in their ideas it consoldiates them into a master list. Excellent and fun tool for keyword brainstorming!
>
> **Rating:** 5 Stars | **Category:** tool

**SERPS.COM KEYWORD TOOL** - https://serps.com/tools/keyword-research/

> Bye bye keyword planner and hello Keyword Tool. SERPS.com has done a great job on this easy-to-use, powerful, and FREE alternative to Google's Keyword Planner.
>
> **Rating:** 5 Stars | **Category:** tool

**UBERSUGGEST** - https://ubersuggest.io/

> Do you love Google suggest (the drop-down suggestions displayed when you type into Google)? It's great for keyword discovery. Ubersuggest is even better - it does

a variety of things to provide all sorts of keyword suggestions. So it's a wonderful keyword discovery tool!

**Rating:** 5 Stars | **Category:** tool

### GOOGLE GLOBAL MARKET FINDER -

http://translate.google.com/globalmarketfinder/g/index.html

This is a new and different spin on the Google keywords tool. You can use it to browse keyword trends by countries, and you can drill down into synonyms based on the primary Google keyword tool. In some ways it's just a cooler, faster way to generate a list of keyword synonyms even if you aren't really interested in geography. Check it out, it's a COOL TOOL.

**Rating:** 5 Stars | **Category:** tool

### GOOGLE ADWORDS KEYWORD PLANNER -

https://adwords.google.com/home/tools/keyword-planner/

Who got the data? Google got the data. Use the Keyword Planner for keyword discovery for both SEO and AdWords, but be sure to know how to use it. Not the easiest user interface, and remember it ONLY gives data for EXACT match types. NOTE: you MUST have a paid account to use.

**Rating:** 4 Stars | **Category:** tool

### SEOCHAT KEYWORD TOOL - http://tools.seochat.com/tools/suggest-tool/

This most awesome keyword suggest tool is like Ubersuggest, but pulls keyword suggestions not just from Google or Bing, but from YouTube, Amazon, etc. Awesome for keyword brainstorming.

**Rating:** 4 Stars | **Category:** tool

### KEYWORD NICHE FINDER - http://wordstream.com/keyword-niche-finder

Really this tool is about finding related keywords. Enter a target keyword and the tool will generate a list of closely related keywords. Then click on any one of those, and the right hand side of the screen will show clusters of those related tools. It is a good tool for keyword discovery, not unlike Google's Wonder Wheel or related searches.

**Rating:** 4 Stars | **Category:** tool

**KEYWORDSPY** - http://www.keywordspy.com/

KeywordSpy currently operates in USA, United Kingdom, Australia and Canada. Through this keyword tool and keyword software, you can perform advanced keyword research and keyword tracking to study what your competitors have been advertising in their AdWords campaigns and other PPC campaigns. You can get complete in-depth analysis, stats, budget, affiliates & ad copies of your competitors.

**Rating:** 4 Stars | **Category:** tool

**SPYFU** - http://www.spyfu.com/

SpyFu will track your ads and competitors ads. Similar to KeywordSpy but not as good. Nonetheless, input a competitor's domain and you can see their ads and some basic information on their keywords and bids.

**Rating:** 4 Stars | **Category:** tool

**KEYWORD FINDER** - https://kwfinder.com/

A very fun, interesting tool to discover keywords. Input some keywords, and get quick ideas for related terms, helper words, and more.

**Rating:** 4 Stars | **Category:** tool

**SEM RUSH** - https://www.semrush.com/

Similar to KeywordSpy, this tool allows you to enter a domain or a competitor, and returns a list of AdWords keywords they are running under as well as their organic keywords. Use it to track a competitor, as well as to generate a keyword list (keyword discovery).

**Rating:** 4 Stars | **Category:** tool

**YOAST KEYWORD SUGGEST TOOL** - https://yoast.com/suggest/

Yet another tool based on Google suggest. The interface is not sexy and pizazzy (is that a word?), but it works.

**Rating:** 3 Stars | **Category:** tool


**KEYWORD TOOL** - http://keywordtool.io

Similar to Ubersuggest, this tool builds upon Google Suggest to provide a list of 'helper' words and phrases. For example, enter insoles and you'll see shoe insoles, insoles for runners, etc. It also provides questions containing the keyword users enter when searching Google and keyword suggestions for YouTube, Bing and Apple App Store. Great for finding helper words as part of keyword research. Additional related data like keyword search volume and CPC requires paid account.

**Rating:** 3 Stars | **Category:** tool


**MERGE WORDS** - http://mergewords.com/

When you build your keywords list, especially for AdWords, you often want to take keywords and combine them into phrases. This is especially true for local search keyword phrases. This tool allows you to enter keywords and generate keyword lists.

**Rating:** 3 Stars | **Category:** tool


**DYNAMIC KEYWORD GENERATOR TOOL** –

http://rustybrick.com/keyword-phrase-tool.php

This tool enables you to enter your primary, secondary and even tertiary keyword phrases separated by comma (,) into the appropriate fields and click Generate Keywords to receive a robust list of keywords to copy and paste into your program of choice. For rank-checking, it makes it easy to generate a longer keyword list.

**Rating:** 3 Stars | **Category:** tool

### SEOCentro Keyword Suggestion Tool –

http://seocentro.com/tools/search-engines/keyword-suggestion.html

> Enter a keyword and it polls Google, Bing, and Yahoo to consolidate their suggestions. Great for keyword discovery as it will suggest close, or related keyword terms.
>
> **Rating:** 3 Stars | **Category:** tool

### SerpStat - http://sg.serpstat.com

> Yet another amazing and fun tool based on Google suggest / suggested searches. Enter your keyword and brainstorm keyword ideas. Allows you to select Google top level domain (e.g., google.com, google.co.uk) for non-US search suggestions.
>
> **Rating:** 3 Stars | **Category:** tool

### Free Negative Keyword Tool - http://wordstream.com/negative-keywords

> Enter your core keyword and this tool gives you 'food for thought' in terms of possible negative keywords. Negative keywords are critical for AdWords, since you pay per click - use this tool to help you find words you DO NOT WANT.
>
> **Rating:** 3 Stars | **Category:** tool

### Content Forest - KeywordKiwi - http://www.contentforest.com/keywordkiwi

> Don't understand the name - is this a play on the infamous 'Kiwi fruit' of New Zealand? No matter, this is a great tool for finding keyword phrases. Enter a keyword, and like Ubersuggest, it gives you a list of related keywords.
>
> **Rating:** 3 Stars | **Category:** tool

### High Paying Keywords - http://www.pagerank.net/high-paying-keywords

> This tool helps identify highest CPC (Cost Per Click) keywords / keyword phrases (i.e., search terms) advertisers are bidding on. This enables you as a website

owner/marketer to understand the most valuable keywords, both for Google AdWords campaigns and/or organic SEO efforts.

**Rating:** 3 Stars | **Category:** tool


### KEYWORD SUGGESTION - http://www.pagerank.net/keyword-suggestion

Yet another tool for keyword discovery. Enter a 'starter' keyword and get suggestions based on volume and value.

**Rating:** 3 Stars | **Category:** tool


### DELETE DUPLICATES KEYWORD TOOL –

http://angular.marketing/free-tools/delete-duplicates

If you are building a long list for rank-checking, or for AdWords input, you often will unknowingly generate duplicates. Then when you pull your reports, they will often not correspond to your original, because rank checker and other tools auto-delete duplicates. Use this tool to prevent this from happening in the first place.

**Rating:** 3 Stars | **Category:** tool

# 2
# AᴅWᴏʀᴅs Tᴏᴏʟs

AdWords, of course, has powerful tools inside the interface – primarily the *Google AdWords Keyword planner* but other tools such as the *Display Planner*, *Ad Preview tool*, etc. In addition, however, there are many wonderful free tools and resources scattered about the Internet that can help you be a more effective advertiser.

Here are the best **free** AdWords tools on the Internet, ranked with the best tools first!

### Tᴀɢ Assɪsᴛᴀɴᴛ ғᴏʀ Cʜʀᴏᴍᴇ - http://tinyurl.com/tagasst

If you're using AdWords and Google Analytics to track conversions, you need to verify you have the right 'tags' running as Javascript on your website. Ask your developer to get the conversion tracking code from AdWords and install on ALL pages of your website. Then use this Chrome extension to double check / verify it actually is there.

**Rating:** 4 Stars | **Category:** tool

### Mᴏᴀᴛ Aᴅ Sᴇᴀʀᴄʜ - https://moat.com/

Want to snoop on competitors? Steal their ad ideas? Enter Moat Ad Search. Enter a competitor name and Moat goes and finds all sorts of ads that they've posted across the Internet. Mainly the Display ads, but excellent to see how a company brainstormed its ad strategy.

**Rating:** 4 Stars | **Category:** tool

### Lᴏᴄᴀʟ Rᴀɴᴋ Cʜᴇᴄᴋɪɴɢ ᴠɪᴀ AᴅWᴏʀᴅs - https://adwords.google.com/apt/AdPreview

This is the OFFICIAL Google AdWords preview tool. But, guess what. You can use this to vary your city location, and check your rank against various cities. If, for example, you are a pizza restaurant serving San Jose, Milpitas, and Santa Clara, you can type in 'Pizza' and see your rank in different cities. You can login to your AdWord account and click Tools - Preview Tool or use this direct link.

**Rating:** 4 Stars | **Category:** tool

### GOOGLE ADWORDS MODIFIED BROAD MATCH KEYWORD TOOL -
http://acquisio.com/ppc/google-adwords-modified-broad-match-keyword-tool

Have a long list of keyword / keyword phrases that did not correctly use the + sign? This tool allows you to copy / paste a list of keywords and then it will automatically add the + sign, so 'presto' you can instantly convert to the more focused broad match with modifier.

**Rating:** 4 Stars | **Category:** tool

### ADWORDS EDITOR - https://adwords.google.com/home/tools/adwords-editor/

AdWords Editor is a free, downloadable (Windows or Mac) application for managing large Google AdWords accounts efficiently. Download campaigns, make changes with powerful editing tools, then upload the changes to AdWords.

**Rating:** 4 Stars | **Category:** tool

### GOOGLE INSIDE ADWORDS BLOG - https://adwords.googleblog.com/

The official blog for Google AdWords. It's more for sophisticated users than for newbies, but - that said - you should pay attention to it if you are spending money with Google.

**Rating:** 4 Stars | **Category:** blog

### LEAD PAGES - https://www.leadpages.net/

Another non-free app, LeadPages allows you to quickly and easily create landing pages (not just for AdWords but for Social Media Campaigns). Then you can split test which ones perform better.

**Rating:** 3 Stars | **Category:** vendor

**SPLIT TESTER BY PERRY MARSHALL** - https://www.perrymarshall.com/splittester/

Is ad one better, or ad two better? AdWords allows you to set up experiments to 'split test' or 'A/B test.' But sometimes it's just as easy to run two ads and plug in the numbers. This tool will then 'do the math.'

**Rating:** 3 Stars | **Category:** tool

**ADWORDS WRAPPER** - http://adwordswrapper.com

Use this tool to take your basic keyword list, and then wrap them with various characters to create each of seven target keyword match types in AdWords (such as quotes for phrase match, and brackets for exact match).

**Rating:** 3 Stars | **Category:** tool

**GOOGLE ADWORDS DISPLAY PLANNER** - https://adwords.google.com/da/DisplayPlanner/Home

Hard to use, but this official Google AdWords tool allows you to input a keyword and see where it might be placed on the Google Display Network, for example, the Sponsored Links section next to search results. In addition, you can use it for keyword research. Must be logged into your Google account to access.

**Rating:** 3 Stars | **Category:** tool

**CLICKFRAUDS.COM** - https://clickfrauds.com/

This service attempts to identify fraudulent IP addresses, and then block them from clicking into your AdWords account.

**Rating:** 3 Stars | **Category:** tool

**MICROSOFT BING ADVERTISING CENTER** - http://advertise.bingads.microsoft.com

Yes, Virginia, there is another search engine besides Google. It's called Bing, and it runs both Bing and Yahoo. And yes, Virginia, you can advertise on Bing, too. It's about 10% of the traffic on Google, on average, though public claims are more like 35%. Try it and see. Often the CPC is lower than on Google, so why not?

**Rating:** 3 Stars | **Category:** resource

**GOOGLE AD GRANTS** - http://www.google.com/grants/

Google Ad Grants is the nonprofit edition of AdWords, Google's online advertising tool. Google Ad Grants empowers nonprofit organizations, through $10,000 per month in in-kind AdWords advertising, to promote their missions and initiatives on Google search engine result pages.

**Rating:** 2 Stars | **Category:** resource

**ADWORDS PREVIEW** - http://adwordspreview.com

Of course, you can log into your AdWords account and preview ads. But this nifty tool lets you do that without logging in, plus provides a preview of what the ad will look like on a mobile device. It also warns you of common violations of Google policy like All Caps. DOES NOT support the new extended text format, however.

**Rating:** 2 Stars | **Category:** tool

**ADWORDS CREATIVE TOOL** –

https://www.hivedigital.com/free-tools/adwords-creative-design/

Use this free tool to pre-generate your AdWords ads. This is a wonderful and easy way to work with a team and generate AdWords ad ideas. Again, does not support the new extended formats.

**Rating:** 2 Stars | **Category:** tool

**CALLRAIL** - https://www.callrail.com/

This is not a free app, but there really aren't any free call tracking apps. Enter CallRail. You can connect it up to your AdWords and generate variable phone numbers to track inbound calls.

**Rating:** 2 Stars | **Category:** vendor

**MATCHPEG ADWORDS GENERATOR** - http://matchpeg.com/misc/adwordsgenerator.asp

Got a list of keywords? Want to create a list of them in phrase match? This nifty tool will do that for you. However, be CAREFUL as it does NOT add the required plus signs for modified broad match!

**Rating:** 2 Stars | **Category:** tool

# 3
# TUTORIALS

Never stop learning! AdWords is complicated, and, while there are many good official Google resources, there are also more objective third party tutorials and information guides available on the Internet. Be a critical reader, however, and don't believe everything that you read, whether on an official Google site or on a third-party blog.

Here are the best **free** AdWords tutorials on the Internet, ranked with the best ones first!

**GOOGLE ADWORDS HELP CENTER** - http://support.google.com/adwords

> Your gateway to easy-to-use lessons about the Google AdWords advertising program. Whether you're just getting started with AdWords, seeking to improve your ad performance, or studying for the Google Advertising Professionals exam, you'll find lessons designed to help you learn at your own pace. You can also read the complete version (with all available lessons).
>
> **Rating:** 5 Stars | **Category:** resource

**ADWORDS YOUTUBE CHANNEL** - https://www.youtube.com/user/learnwithgoogle

> Official Google AdWords channel. Learn from the horse's mouth how to advertise on AdWords, why advertise, etc. Of course, be a bit skeptical as it is by Google, about Google, and ultimately for Google!
>
> **Rating:** 4 Stars | **Category:** resource

**GOOGLE PARTNERS HELP CENTER** - https://support.google.com/partners

Google partners is Google's platform for agencies and consultants, particularly for AdWords. However, you can 'join' as an individual and thereby get access to many wonderful FREE Google AdWords learning resources. If you are a serious learner with respect to AdWords, this is a great way to go behind the scenes and learn even more about AdWords.

**Rating:** 4 Stars | **Category:** resource

**GOOGLE ADWORDS COMMUNITY** - https://en.adwords-community.com

This is the official Google AdWords community group, wherein users post questions and get answers from Googlers or other AdWords gurus on AdWords. It's a bit of a free-for-all but useful if you have a burning question about AdWords! Just remember that these are Google forums, so things can be on the salesy side.

**Rating:** 4 Stars | **Category:** resource

**GOOGLE ADWORDS ON FACEBOOK** - https://www.facebook.com/ENadwords/

Google's official AdWords page on Facebook. If you are into AdWords, then you should 'like' the Google's AdWords page on Facebook to receive information as Google makes it available here.

**Rating:** 3 Stars | **Category:** resource

**GOOGLE ADWORDS ON TWITTER** - https://twitter.com/adwords

Can't get enough official AdWords information? Up late at night? Follow official Google AdWords on Twitter!

**Rating:** 3 Stars | **Category:** resource

**FROM BEGINNER TO PRO: 21 FREE ADWORDS TUTORIALS FOR 2016** - https://agencyanalytics.com/blog/adwords-tutorials

Christian Sculthorp published this all-in-one, massive cornucopia of blog posts and tutorials to AdWords. It's a bit much, and the quality is VERY uneven in terms of the referenced resource. But it's organized by category / level and, if you use it in combination with more hefty resources like books, you can learn a lot, quickly. Be a critical reader, however; don't believe everything you read.

**Rating:** 2 Stars | **Category:** resource

### ADWORDS TUTORIAL BY GOOGLE -
https://support.google.com/adwords/answer/6146252

Get ready to learn Google's official policies and suggestions on AdWords. Yes, it's propaganda! Yes, it's overly optimistic! But, yes, if you're serious about AdWords you can, and should, learn from the Google directly.

**Rating:** 2 Stars | **Category:** resource

### THINK WITH GOOGLE - https://www.thinkwithgoogle.com/

This flashy, very Madison Avenue ad agency guide is a gateway to fun and sometime informative studies by Google about Google, and about Internet advertising and marketing in general. It pushes AdWords, of course, but still has a wealth of fun stuff about Internet marketing.

**Rating:** 2 Stars | **Category:** resource

# 4

# BOOKS

Our philosophy at the JM Internet Group is to be transparent. Yes, we have amazing books, and yes, we'll soon have our own *AdWords Workbook*. However, there are a few great books available on Amazon, and the smartest strategy is to read EVERYTHING you can about AdWords, not to mention Bing and/or Yahoo.

Here are the best **books** on AdWords, ranked with the most highly recommended first!

### ULTIMATE GUIDE TO GOOGLE ADWORDS: HOW TO ACCESS 100 MILLION PEOPLE IN 10 MINUTES - http://amzn.to/2mu3obh

Perry Marshall and Mike Rhodes bring us one of the true Bibles on Google AdWords. That's the good news. The bad news is that this book was written in 2014, and it's badly in need of an update. It's a deep-dive into everything AdWords, and definitely worth reading, but you have to constantly check to see what's changed, and what's not, in terms of Google AdWords. The strategies and concepts, however, will stand much of the test of time.

**Rating:** 3 Stars | **Category:** book

### ADVANCED GOOGLE ADWORDS - http://amzn.to/2mu2GsT

Brad Geddes brings us what I would call the second 'Bible' on AdWords. But like the book by Perry Marshall it's terribly out-of-date being written in 2014. Read it for strategy and concepts, but please check and double-check to make sure that various technical details remain accurate vis-a-vis AdWords.

**Rating:** 3 Stars | **Category:** book

**ESSENTIAL ADWORDS: THE QUICK AND DIRTY GUIDE (INCLUDING TRICKS GOOGLE WON'T TELL YOU)** - http://amzn.to/2jXIwWB

Kyle Sulerud brings us, 'Essential AdWords: The Quick and Dirty Guide is a hard-hitting, no-B.S. guide on how to drastically improve your business using AdWords. There are no bells-and-whistles'

**Rating:** 3 Stars | **Category:** book

**GOOGLE ADWORDS FOR BEGINNERS: A DO-IT-YOURSELF GUIDE TO PPC ADVERTISING** - http://amzn.to/2mu32jd

Corey Rabazinski brings us a very basic book on AdWords. In his words, 'Learn how to increase web traffic and sales using Google AdWords. Google's AdWords platform enables you to create pay-per-click advertisements that appear as 'sponsored links' when someone searches for content related to your product or service. You bid for the position to place your ad, and you only pay when someone clicks. It's that simple. If used correctly, AdWords can garner higher targeted traffic, which in turn will increase your conversion rates and profits. So, AdWords will definitely help your business, but you have no idea how to utilize them.'

**Rating:** 2 Stars | **Category:** book

**GOOGLE ADWORDS SECRETS EXPOSED: HOW YOU CAN NAVIGATE THE COMPLICATED WORLD OF ONLINE MARKETING AND COME OUT ON TOP** - http://amzn.to/2jXnpDQ

Jeremy Overturf writes, ' In these pages you'll discover: - Why knowing your target market is vital to Adwords - How to discover which items are a good fit and which aren't - How to track and test ads and why it makes all the difference - Why most people don't test headlines enough and give up too soon - How to schedule your ads so you're not spending when you're not open'

**Rating:** 2 Stars | **Category:** book

**THE SMART MARKETER'S GUIDE TO GOOGLE ADWORDS** - http://amzn.to/2jXwr3C

Noa Eshed says, 'The aim of this book is to provide marketers with a detailed and easy to understand explanation on how to create, measure and scale a Google AdWords campaign. We suggest that even if you are working with an agency, you invest a few hours to understanding the basics. On a grand strategic level, this book will help you become a better marketer, focusing on smartly channeling your marketing efforts to platforms where you can track your progress and success.'

**Rating:** 2 Stars | **Category:** book

# SURVEY OFFER

**CLAIM YOUR $10 REBATE OR FREE BOOK! HERE'S HOW –**

1. Visit http://jmlinks.com/survey.
2. Take a short, simple survey about the book.
3. Indicate whether you want a $10.00 rebate or a free copy of one of Jason's other books on SEO / Social Media Marketing / Job Search & Career-building.

**WE WILL THEN –**

- Rebate you the $10.00, or send you a free copy of one of the other books.

**~ $10 REBATE OFFER ~**

**~ LIMITED TO ONE PER CUSTOMER ~**

**EXPIRES: 4/1/2017**

**SUBJECT TO CHANGE WITHOUT NOTICE**

**GOT QUESTIONS? CALL 800-298-4065**

Other books by Jason McDonald

**SEO Fitness Workbook**

**Social Media Marketing Workbook**

Available on Amazon and more information at https://www.jm-seo.org/.

www.ingramcontent.com/pod-product-compliance
Lightning Source LLC
LaVergne TN
LVHW060149070326
832902LV00018B/3031